Greece Chunder Dutt

Cherry Stones

Greece Chunder Dutt

Cherry Stones

ISBN/EAN: 9783743344488

Manufactured in Europe, USA, Canada, Australia, Japa

Cover: Foto ©ninafisch / pixelio.de

Manufactured and distributed by brebook publishing software (www.brebook.com)

Greece Chunder Dutt

Cherry Stones

CHERRY STONES,

BY

GREECE C. DUTT.

"Trifles light as air,"
Shakespeare.

CALCUTTA:
PRINTED BY P. S D'ROZARIO AND COMPANY, 12, WATERLOO STREET.

1879.

DEDICATED

TO

My Wife,

WITH MY LOVE.

CONTENTS.

SONNETS.

		page.
I.—Sonnet		1
II.—Sonnet (At Thirty-five) ...		2
III.—Sonnet		3
IV.—Sonnet		4
V.—Sonnet		5
VI.—Sonnet		6
VII.—Sonnet (On the fly leaf of Alford's New Testament)		7
VIII.—Sonnet (Revelations, II. 7.) ...		8
IX.—Sonnet (Philippians, I. 29.) ...		9
X.—Sonnet		10
XI.—Sonnet (Despondency) ...		11
XII.—Sonnet		12
XIII.—Sonnet (Malta)		13
XIV.—Sonnet (On the fly-leaf of Elliot's Horæ Apocalypticæ) ...		14
XV.—Sonnet		15
XVI.—Sonnet (A mission station) ...		16
XVII.—Sonnet		17
XVIII.—Sonnet (Khan Saheb's house, College Square)		18
XIX.—Sonnet (Bligh Sands) ...		19
XX.—Sonnet (Gibraltar) ...		20
XXI.—Sonnet (To * *)		21

CONTENTS.

	page.
XXII.—Sonnet (Aboukir)	22
XXIII.—Sonnet	23
XXIV.—Sonnet (Converts' Home.——Street)	24
XXV.—Sonnet (To——)	25
XXVI.—Sonnet (Burra Bazar)	26
XXVII.—Sonnet (The Nepali Peasant)	27
XXVIII.—Sonnet (Off Aden)	28
XXIX.—Sonnet (Extr. Cannabis Indicæ)	29
XXX.—Sonnet (Near Goa)	30
XXXI.—Sonnet (The Wilkie Gallery)	31
XXXII.—Sonnet (On a small Pine wood box)	32
XXXIII.—Sonnet	33
XXXIV.—Sonnet (To J. C.)	34
XXXV.—Sonnet	35
XXXVI.—Sonnet (Punkabaree)	36
XXXVII.—Sonnet	37
XXXVIII.—Sonnet	38
XXXIX.—Sonnet (Near Nynee Thal)	39
XL.—Sonnet	40
XLI.—Sonnet	41
XLII.—Sonnet (Chini in Koonawar)	42
XLIII.—Sonnet	43
XLIV.—Sonnet (Terai—Distant prospect of the Hills)	44
XLV.—Sonnet	45
XLVI.—Sonnet (Rapids of the Balasun)	46
XLVII.—Sonnet (1858)	47
XLVIII.—Sonnet	48

CONTENTS.

iii

	page.
XLIX.—Sonnet (In Summer) ...	49
L.—Sonnet ...	50
LI.—Sonnet (Source of the Sone)	51
LII.—Sonnet ...	52
LIII.—Sonnet ...	53
LIV.—Sonnet (Sacoontala) ...	54
LV.—Sonnet (1871) ...	55
LVI.—Sonnet (To a Dove) ...	56

MISCELLANEOUS PIECES.

On an old Romaunt,	59
Absence,	62
Reminiscences of Travel. The Straits of Jubal,	64
Shadows,	67
A Charade,	68
Stanzas,	70
Solitude,	73
Sunjogta,	75
Fire Hunters,	78
A Charade,	80
Samarsi,	81
Stanzas,	83
Stanzas,	84
No. 13, Manicktolla Street,	86
The Maid of Roopnagore,	87
Stanzas,	89

CONTENTS.

	page.
Stanzas,	90
The Mill,	91
Lines,	93
Die Weisze Fraü,	94
On board S.S. "Retribution" off Cape Fiolant,	97
Lines,	98
Sita,	99
The Brook,	101
Coco Palms,	103
Margarete,	104
Water Fowl,	105
Near Seoni,	107
Notes.	

SONNETS.

SONNETS.

I.

SONNET.

'God seeth all' the Hebrew psalmist taught.
   How dreadful that the Just and Holy One
   Scans every moment what our hands have done,
Our hearts have nursed, our wayward feet have sought!
Yet to the precious few who have been bought
   With the dear Blood of His Eternal Son,
   Who the white robe of righteousness have won,
Oh, heart-assuring and consoling thought!
Whate'er their guilt, whate'er their deeds have been,
   Firm rests their faith on Him, nor fears to fall,
Though oft the accuser comes, unwatched, unseen,
   To prompt a doubt, they feel God seeth all;
Deliberate is the love that deems them clean,
   Without repentance are the gifts and call.

II.

SONNET.

(AT THIRTY-FIVE.)

The days of our years are three score years and ten. —PSALM XC. 10.

As visions sweet of old familiar trees,
  Of English downs with sheepcotes sprinkled o'er,
  Of toddling children by the school-house door,
Greet the lone whaler on Canadian seas,
What time, his cruise complete, the freshening breeze
  Veers round his wave-worn bark for Albyn's shore,
  And, though the surf chides loud off Labrador,
Awaken tender hopes, keen sympathies,
Even so sweet dreams of friends in raiment white
  My spirit greet, though anxious fears chide near,
Dreams of great mansions warm with love and light,
  Of golden harps and palms and waters clear,
  Of angel heads bent meekly down to pray :
Life's ship has veered ! I sail for home to-day !

III.

SONNET.

On autumn eves I love in listless mood,
    While yet the west retains its golden hue,
    And the leaves whisper and the stars are few,
To saunter leisurely by lake and wood,
And mark the dorhawk and its tawny brood,
    Half lost by distance to the aching view,
    With restless wings and eager hum pursue
The drowsy beetle over plain and flood.
Or if perchance chill rains sweep down the dell,
    By the warm hearth reclined, I love to hear
    My true love read, in accents silvery clear,
    (While ruffian blasts howl o'er the moors forlorn)
Of Jesus musing by the desert well,
    Or sad Ruth gleaning in Judean corn.

IV.

SONNET.

In my life's morn where now a palace high
   Rears its proud arches and pilasters light,
   Enchased with costly stones of stainless white,
A lonely heath reposed, gorse-clad and dry;
An aged Moslem owned a hut hard by,
   A friend of legends store, whose nimble sight
   Could oft, (men said), in lonely lanes by night
The fairy queen, and elfin court descry!
Blest morn of life! sweet time of song and play!
   What soulfelt joys were thine! What blissful dreams!
I long believed, from regions far away
   Of pleasant shadows and purpereal gleams,
That old man's magic art could gems purvey,
   As bright as frost wreaths lit with morning beams!

V.

SONNET.

Keep me apart in safe obscurity,
   In closest covert hide my lowly nest,
   And guide my footsteps, kindest Lord and best,
Through desert places to the realms on high,
For otherwise, so weak and frail am I,
   Vain aims, ambitious hopes, shall cross my breast,
   And I shall harbour schemes that breed unrest,
Forget Thy Name, and worldward drift and die.
In mercy grant no pitying face but Thine
   To cheer my trembling soul in solitude,
And let the Life of Life in me and mine,
   When clouds and darkness o'er the pathway brood,
Unnoticed burn, as burns at eve's decline
   The hermit's taper in a pathless wood.

VI.

SONNET.

Should I feel faint if in a neighbour's field
    The good seed of the Word bears hundredfold,
    Or if the talent which in trust we hold
In skilful hands ten times its value yield?
I know not, but my lowly heart is steeled
    Against all rivalry : I am not bold
In merit's race : my sins are manifold.
Be Thou, O Lord, the weak one's strength and shield!
Like the broad cistern can the cup brim o'er,
    And he who gained two pounds rejoicing went
To share Christ's bliss, with him who passed before.
    Small though the increase be which God has sent
In mercy to my field and treasure store,
I rest secure in hope and calm content.

VII.

SONNET.

(ON THE FLY-LEAF OF ALFORD'S NEW TESTAMENT.)

The shepherds then gave them the glass to look: and they looked and saw something like the gate, and also some of the glory of the place.—BUNYAN.

Long had we roamed with footsteps faint and frail,
   To reach the land of joy and love and light;
   The wilderness was drear, and dark the night,
Sheep-track and ford lay wrapt in vapours pale;
The floods had risen, and with an angry wail
   Swept chafing over roots and boulders white;
   The lightning's gleam but mocked the aching sight,
And doleful murmurs filled the blustering gale.
Dear Guide, in seasonable hour thy lore,
   Like the clear glass by wondering Christian seen,
Revealed the cheerful trees that shadow o'er
   Beulah's trim orchard walks—the path serene
Of crystal waters, and the city door,
   With dome and minaret crowned and foliage green.

VIII.

SONNET.

(REVELATION II. 17.)

Oft have I seen a pebble rough and dark,
   Made smooth by skilful hands with patient care,
   Discover branching veins of beauty rare,
And glorious bars, and specks like those which mark
The downy breastplate of the dainty lark,
   Or blending hues which safely may compare
   With those refracted, when the woods are bare,
From trembling icicles, or from Iris' arc.
So shall my soul, Father of love and light,
   Cleansed with atoning Blood, and heavenly Flame,
Become a gem, though erst in woful plight,
   And foul with sordid lust, and selfish aim ;
A tablet smooth, heart shaped, and gleaming white,
   Fit for the inscription of the Secret Name.

IX.

SONNET.

(PHILIPPIANS I. 29.)

Meek snowdrops, couriers of auspicious spring,
  Ye who with faithfulness from day to day,
  Like hardy veterans in close array,
Brave the rude buffets of the north wind's wing;
Ye who with loyal trust tenacious cling,
  In rain and frost, upon the parent spray,
  And wait, in hope assured, May's genial sway,
Strength to my soul in peril's hour ye bring.
For ye the lowliness and courage high,
  The stern resolve, the constancy of mood
Of suffering Christians aptly typify—
  Christians close-linked in love and brotherhood,
Like those who side by side at Philippi
  Bore the world's hate with noble fortitude.

X.

SONNET.

A mighty thrill of rapture stirred my heart,
   When from the Bosphorus, arrayed in light,
   The Sultan's city started up to sight,
Spire, column, terrace, street and crowded mart,
Seemed fairer far than aught enchanter's art
   Called up in yore. Far off like seagulls white,
   Winging through sun and shade their restless flight,
A hundred glancing sails appeared to meet and part;
I gazed, and thought if joy like mine is found
   From earthly sight in hearts benumbed with care,
What are *their* transports who for Zion bound,
   With angel guides, first see in upper air
The groves of massy foliage, minarets tall,
The everlasting dome and golden wall.

XI.

SONNET.

DESPONDENCY.

I feel like one unnerved by keen distress,
   I care not either to converse or pray,
   My soul seems duller than the senseless clay,
And vague distorted dreams my brain possess,
My very thoughts o'ercome by Idleness,
   Forbear disheartened to expand or play,
   And like an oilless lamp with lambent ray,
My Faith, ah woe is me! shines less and less;
Yet once bright Hopes and stedfast Aims were mine,
   And Fancies jocund as the gales of spring,
And sage Content that made my face to shine,
   And Industry best charm for sorrow's sting.
Oh Christ! in mercy hear a sinner's cry,
Renew my inward man before I die.

XII.

SONNET.

As the caged linnet, though on dainties fed,
    Turns wild with joy and beats the ruthless bars,
    When the faint perfume from the market cars
Of ripened fruit at early morn is shed;
Or when a fleecy cloud appears o'erhead,
    And tells, 'mid London's smoke and deafening jars,
    Of chasing shadows over downs and scaurs,
And reaper bands by rich sheaves islanded,—
Even so my heart, though here my pathway lies
    Through pleasant places, bounds with wild delight,
When in the prophecy of prophecies
    I reach the realms that know not joyless night,
Where healing leaves a chequered shadow fling,
And crystal waters from the white throne spring.

XIII.

SONNET.

MALTA.

How oft our souls, against the senses, dare
   Link opposite extremes! When first my sight
   Met Malta's coast, the wayward sea shone bright,
That laves her terraced cliffs and headlands fair :
While her tall steeples, carved with skilful care,
   Her zig-zag ramparts, and her villas white,
   Superbly varnished by the noonday light,
Gleamed like pure silver in the smokeless air :
But o their lustre to my inward eye,
   Was a weird mirror in whose depths again,
It summoned boldly from tho years gone by,
   The dismal shore obscured by ceaseless rain,
And the dark rollers topped with livid foam,
That Paul encountered on his way to Rome.

XIV.

SONNET.

ON THE FLY LEAF OF ELLIOT'S HORÆ APOCALYPTICÆ,
1. COR. 2. 9.

A careworn mourner on the earth, the soul,
  Has no conception of the joys that wait,
  The ransomed Church beyond the pearly gate,
By Life's unfading tree, its destined goal ;
The glorious Future is a mystic scroll,
  And none of Adam's race, or small or great,
  May in the torpor of this dim estate
The lofty secrets of its text unroll :
E'en to the wise the words that St. John wrote,
  (Oh hard obdurate heart unapt to hear,)
Sound fainter than the vagrant cuckoo's note
  Sounds 'mid the glaciers to the mountaineer,
When first the breeze breathes soft from vales remote,
  And snowdrops pale, in sheltered clefts appear.

XV.

SONNET.

Baronial walls which lofty elms embower,
 Rich summer fruits, and waters sparkling clear,
 Smooth-shaven lawns, where browse the dappled deer,
A stone soft veined, a song, an opening flower,
Colours and leaves, can stir my heart with power ;
 And there are trees and streams in Paradise,
 And fruits and leaves, and gems of dazzling dyes,
Far-stretching wall, and gate, and guarded tower :
But not for these in sadness here I pine,
 For these my spirit frets not to be free,
But where hymns rise, and angel faces shine,
 There do I yearn in spirit, silently,
To stand and gaze upon His eyes benign,
 Whose heart felt pity for a worm like me.

XVI.

SONNET.

(A MISSION STATION.)

Blest be the hands that reared with patient skill
  This seemly chapel by the brooklet's fall,
    These trim-kept orchards, barns, and homesteads small,
And devious gravel walks o'er slope and hill,
That girdled with smooth stepping-stones the rill,
  And fenced the pastures with a leafy wall
    Of closely-planted palms and poplars tall,
Where timid herds securely range at will.
For God works surely with the meek, the true,
  Who spite of weak beginnings lack not power
To hope and pray—who in the swart seed view
  The glorious hues that flush the dainty flower :
Whose living faith in heathen men descry
White vested kings, and priests that never die.

XVII.

SONNET.

O deem him not the sport of carking care,
   Or sullen humours, or distractions rude,
   A hardened wretch, upon whose bosom brood
Mistrustful pride, and leaden-eyed despair,
Who lays in sorest straits his counsels bare
   To God alone ; who covets solitude—
   Whose soul disdains, with stubborn hardihood,
The amaranth crown with mortal help to wear.
His are ripe hopes who waits on none save God,
   And joys serene, undimmed by earthly stains.
I often see (rambling at eve abroad
   In golden autumn, over hills and plains)
Pure waters well in clefts, which men ne'er trod,
   And luscious berries lurk in lonely lanes.

XVIII.

SONNET.

(KHAN SAHIB'S HOUSE, NEAR COLLEGE SQUARE.)

A Persian's mansion, near the Vacool trees,
  That bound the College green, with its array
  Of Ethiop porters, oft in boyhood's day,
When Fancy wove the subtlest webs with ease,
Recalled the age when Sinbad ploughed the seas
  With bales of spicery from far Cathay.
  It was a stately pile of granite grey,
With carved pilasters, and quaint balconies.
Exotic plants with gaudy blossoms starred
  Its terraces ; a marble dolphin flung
  In the wide court, a limpid column high ;
The windows of the upper rooms were barred,
  But through the lattice-work, with creepers hung,
  Glanced now and then an arm, or lustrous eye.

XIX.

SONNET.

BLIGH SANDS.

If thy soul joys to watch the swelling sail,
    When the dark hull is scarce discerned from land,
    Or from a cliff, whose base on either hand,
Breasts the green swell that harbingers a gale,
To hear the curlew's cry, the wild swan's wail,
    Echoed from reedy isles that skirt the strand,
    What time at eve, o'er rock and darkening sand,
The lonely light-house flings its radiance pale;
Or if wide spreading downs thy spirit please,
    And purple hills o'er which the spires and vanes
Of some proud manor rise, half hid by trees,
    To whose thick branches the sea breeze complains
In whispers hoarse,—o feast thy sight and heart
On this fair fruit of Turner's matchless art.

XX.

SONNET.

GIBRALTAR.

The flag that here floats proudly in the air,
    The silent warders on the ramparts white,
    The guns that hide in sheltered nooks from sight,
Or from the seaward scarp, their chosen lair,
Frown on the waters with an iron stare,
    The rock-cut embrasures ablaze at night,
    The mole—the ships—the keep's commanding height,
All speak of stern resolve, and watchful care.
For leagued in arms should Europe rise once more,
    To question on this steep the Lion's reign,
Swift must the deadly hail of battles pour,
    As on the day when baffled France and Spain
Beheld their vaunted ships in flames ashore,
    Or drifting helpless on the stormy main.

XXI.

SONNET.

TO * *

Unmoved by fears through life's drear waste to go,
  Is thine oh lady of the downcast eyes,
  For thine the settled Will, the Hopes that rise
From lavish Faith ; how smooth the tranquil flow
Of thy calm hours. What fagrant blossoms grow
  In the fair garden of thy mind that lies
    Fenced with pure thoughts, whose stedfast strength defies
The fitful gusts, our fiercest passions blow :
And they who mark thy unobtrusive grace,
  Thy saintly pensiveness, thy modest pride,
Oft to the raptured heart the vision call,
  Of Mary, watching by the manger's side,
Or Eve, in Eden, ere the primal fall,
  Serene and silent in a shady place.

XXII.

SONNET.

ABOUKIR.

The fleet made Egypt as the sun went down,
   Fringing the golden West with crimson flame,
   And as its dauntless Chief resolved to claim
That night from France her wreath and beaming crown,
By Bequier's frowning cape and sand spits brown,
   With swelling sail in loose array it came,
   Baffling with matchless skill, the foeman's aim,
Its beacon light, Britannia's past renown.
Then rose in air the battle's dreadful roar,
   The guns flashed fiercely from each bloodstained deck,
And hurtling fragments vast o'er sea and shore,
   The grand explosion rent the Orient's wreck,
While Justice smiled, as spread the lurid glare,
To see that France lay prostrate in despair.

XXIII.

SONNET.

There is a natural chapel on the hill
   Near Dymok, worthier far than aught,
   For solemn worship, mortal hands have wrought,
A grotto green with moss, secure and still.
Fast by its portal sweeps a sparkling rill
   Of lucid waters, by the small birds sought,
   When fervid June with bluebells paints the spot,
And joyous songs the listening hawthorns thrill.
Like the low harmony of morning dreams,
   The wind there murmurs through an old oak tree,
And light, as solemn as a church beseems,
   Falls at high noon, through green leaves, placidly,
Pensive and holy as the light that gleams,
   In the lone caves beneath the roaring sea.

XXIV.

SONNET.

CONVERT'S HOME.——STREET.

The humblest minnow in its native stream,
   Breasting the freshets, or at careless play,
   Where stones and dancing flags the tide delay,
I hold more lovely than the shoals that gleam
In radiant globes of crystal, though they seem
   Like living gems, or elves in loose array,
   Whose polished corslets, and brigandines gay,
Flash back with usury the pale moon's beam :
The hardy snowdrop that untended blows,
   By hedgerow paths, when winter rules the sky,
I deem too, sweeter than the hot-house rose,
   That droops dejected at the north wind's sigh ;
And thus these lofty walls, this verdant close,
I pass to-day, nor feel my heart swell high.

XXV.

SONNET.

TO ⸻

On cloudless eves lone sitting on the ground
  By the brook's marge, beneath the willows green,
  Or by my cottage fire when winds are keen,
Listening with careless ear the light rain sound
Against the panes, or tracing chasms profound,
  Rocks, towns, and trees the glowing bars between,
  When I contrast, O Friend, thy life serene
With the rude discord of the world around,
Thee, with a land-locked haven I compare,
  That sleeps unruffled when wild tempests blow,
Or a lone palm amid the deserts bare,
  Whose ripened nuts in golden clusters glow,
Or yet a lighted window when the air
  Is filled at night with drifting wreaths of snow.

XXVI.

SONNET.

BURRA BAZAR.

Through crowded alleys which o'er head display
   A tortuous seam of pure unclouded sky,
   Past groups of glorious mosques and pagods high,
And bubbling basins crowned with garlands gay,
Oft, ere the school bell rang, this dim archway
   I sought in youth (how swift Time courses by!)
   For top, or ball, or beads of gaudy dye,
Or haply, dreams of times long past away:
In sooth, a fitter spot to realize
   The days when Bagdad held Al Raschid dear,
Is not on earth; for bales of goodly size,
   Embroidered scarfs, and jewelled dirks lie here,
And in the stalls arrayed in turbans green,
   White-bearded men with amber pipes are seen.

XXVII.

SONNET.

THE NEPALI PEASANT.

Nursed with the eagle's brood, afar from men,
  A simple hind, the hardy mountaineer
  Lives on wild herbs and waters sparkling clear
And chestnuts gathered in the bosky glen;
Yet is he happy as the lonely wren
  Warbling by fits her hymns of lofty cheer,
  At shut of eve on Kanchun's summit drear,
Hid in her nest from blasts and human ken.
Nor lacks he patriot zeal to keep his land
  Of snow and fog and chasms yawning wide,
From foreign insult,—witness that bold band
  Of England's sons, who, vainly struggling, died—
Urged to the contest by the rash command
  Of careless rulers—by Gillespie's side.

XXVIII.

SONNET.

OFF ADEN.

The helpful lascar scans with ravished eye,
   The hardy fisher's unpretending cot,
   On this stupendous coast where trees are not,
But grim volcanic cliffs, abrupt and dry;
For 'tis his faith that Labor may defy
   Nature's worst frowns,—that hearts with courage fraught,
   Find in the roughest waste,—the sternest spot,
Enough our vital wants to satisfy:
And oft when leisure serves, he gaily notes
   The simple implements that lie around
Its rough built walls—nets, jars, and bamboo floats
   With strips of pliant cane securely bound,
Or marks the thin smoke from its roof aspire,
Like a dull snake devoid of strength and fire.

XXIX.

SONNET.

EXTR: CANNABIS INDICÆ.

This magic dust can wake to ecstacy
   The toil-worn sense, and banish irksome care,
   Yea, rive the iron chain of fixed despair,
And waft the spirit, buoyant——hopeful——free,
O'er earth and ocean's wide immensity,
   To Dreamland's distant strand, on wings of air:
   Wouldst thou have visions exquisite and rare?
Taste it, and lo! thy wondering eyes shall see
Rich wreaths of vivid green, and silver bells,
   Fair laughing brows which sparkling coins adorn,
Great groups of pendant spars, and red-lipped shells,
   And fairy flowers, such as the frost at morn
Paints on the gleaming panes with fingers white,
And broad colures, and bars of golden light.

XXX.

SONNET.

NEAR GOA.

I love this churchyard by the voiceful sea,
    With its low wall, its heaps of mouldered stone.
    Its shattered urns, its effigies o'erthrown,
Its velvet turf, its gloomy banyan tree,
Its timid bats that flit mysteriously
    Like ghosts at nightfall, and its bell whose tone
    Reminds the pilgrim as he plods alone,
That Time glides onward to Eternity :
For here they rest, whose patient fortitude,
    Delivered Xavier from the heathen's hand,
Who fought with Albuquerque the pirates rude,
    Of wild Socotra, girt with surf and sand,
Who watched the needle undepressed by fear,
In stedfast Gama's bark, when rocks loomed near.

XXXI.

SONNET.

THE WILKIE GALLERY.

Sublime at need,—minute as were of yore,
   The Flemish Masters, Wilkie stands apart
   Among our artists for consummate art,
'Tis his, with matchless grace to ope the door
Of household sympathies; he dares explore
   Passion's extremest moods, and keenly dart
   Through the dim chambers of a careworn heart,
Light, on what nestles at its inmost core:
Witness the "Breakfast," with its gleaming tray,
   It's cheerful parlour, and it's table spread
With homespun damask, white as mountain snow,
And witness too the monk's despairing woe,
   In the "Confession," as convulsed with dread,
He grasps his elder's hand to kneel and pray.

XXXII.

SONNET

ON A SMALL PINE-WOOD BOX.

When parching winds blow fierce from tropic seas,
   And my soul faints with heat and glaring light,
   The magic perfume of this casket white,
Transports me far to Simla's shady trees :
I hear the murmur of the golden bees,
   Now lost in flowers, now glancing back to sight,
   And the wren's whistle on the lonely height,
And harvests rustling in the autumn breeze.
Above, around, start grove and hawthorn brake,
   And peaceful homes, and spots of open sky,
Bright as the glimpses of a winding lake,
   Pure, blue, transparent, sleeping silently,
Embosomed among mountains that partake
   The boundless desert's deep tranquillity.

XXXIII.

SONNET.

I see fair figures in my dreams at night,
  Such as Murillo's heaven-taught pencil drew.
  Faces irradiate with the holy dew
Of innocence—a music exquisite,
Like that which Zephyr wakes with fingers light,
  From harp Æolian for Titania's crew,
  When autumn leaves the forest paths bestrew,
Floats round these visions as they swim to sight.
I see Rebecca by the fountain's side,
  Meek Ruth amid the reapers walking slow,
Fair Rachel frowning in her beauty's pride,
  Sad Hannah in the temple's portico,
The Virgin musing at sweet eventide,
  And my own mother dear, in robes of snow.

XXXIV.

SONNET.

TO J. C.

Dear friend, meek traveller in the narrow way!
   Thou that with lowly heart and faithfulness—
   Careless of good report and ill—dost press
Thy journey forward to the realms of day:
Thou that like Sarah casting care away,
   Hast left friends, mother, childhood's peaceful home,
   And with thy cross outside the gate hast come,
God be thy strength and guide, thy shield and stay!
Oh, may I see thee, when the swelling cry
   Of thronging myriads on each shore and isle
Proclaims the Bridegroom's advent from the sky,
   (While white-robed angels march in endless file),
In joyous welcome o'er the crowd lift high,
   Thy brightly-burning lamp with tearful smile!

XXXV.

SONNET.

'Our sorest trials, our severest woes,
   Are nothing to the glory that shall be.'
So spake the foremost, trustiest soldier—he
Who fought for Christ with more than mortal foes,
Who near his chequered life's pathetic close
   Rejoiced to fall, and cross in hand to die.
Oh, mighty faith, that could the mystery
Of life resolve and sordid fears compose!
What hopes, what dreams were his! what visions bright
   Of things we long for! plumes, and glistening wings,
And bands of worshippers arrayed in white,
   And watered gardens, and unfailing springs,
And bridal mirth, and kings with offerings sweet,
By guarded gate and stream and shady street.

XXXVI.

SONNET.

PUNKABAREE.

How sweet 'twere here an anchorite to dwell,
   Here in the presence of this white cascade,
   To muse at noon beneath this grateful shade,
With bead and crucifix to haunt this cell;
Fresh wholesome fruits to gather in the dell,
   At early morn what time broad lights invade
   The dew-gemmed coverts of the peaceful glade,
And listening silence broods o'er rock and fell;
With solemn cheer to mark at eve on high
   The stars leap forth, to lie on this smooth stone
Strewed with crisp leaves, and hear the owlet's cry
   Borne on the breeze from crag and cavern lone,
Or close in balmy sleep the languid eye,
   Lulled by the deep-voiced Teesta's soothing tone.

XXXVII.

SONNET.

Like a great temple built to Nature's God,
   Kanchun uprears his stately form in air;
   A crown of stainless snow his turrets wear,
And virgin forests o'er the basement nod.
No tourist seeks him, but the fissures broad
   That trench his ample side, the glaciers bright
   On his wide slopes, are sacred to my sight;
The ground on which he stands is sainted sod.
When life hangs heavy, and sharp cares and woes
   Vex the smooth current of my tranquil mind,
While sunset bathes his loftiest cone in light,
How often peaceful thoughts and calm delight,
   And soothing hopes, and sadness mild I find,
In his rich colours and his still repose!

XXXVIII.

SONNET.

My Alpine villa on Hemmaven's brow,
   A prospect wide commands of vale and hill,
   Green sunny pastures, and meand'ring rill,
Dark dwindled woods, and blank untrodden snow;
Cool bracing breezes round it freely blow.
   And naught disturbs the slumber soft and still
   That laps the grounds, save when with tuneful bill
Her song the stock-dove trills in accents low.
Hard by, the Guardian Genius of the place,
   A lonely pinetree by a noiseless stream,
It's massy foliage lifts with matchless grace,
   Fit canopy from scorching noonday beam,
For Dian panting from the toilsome chase,
   Or lonely poet lost in mazy dream.

XXXIX.

SONNET.

NEAR NYNEE THAL.

How rich the prospect from this moss-grown seat!
    The vine-clad cottage in the warm recess
    Shines like a palm tree of the wilderness,
When lone Arabia pants with torrid heat.
Below, where from the lake the hills retreat,
    And the wild strawberry woos the sun's caress,
    How calm the cattle lie—how motionless!
Lulled by faint warblings from Deoban's feet.
How smooth the fields appear by yonder rill,
    Where 'neath the shelter of an old oak tree,
    'Mid snow-white sheep, on green turf lazily,
    His rod in hand, the patient angler lies,
    Arch, innocent, with ruddy cheeks, and eyes
Like its translucent pools serene and still.

XL.

SONNET.

Landour I saw when winter ruled the sky ;
   Fled were the laughing flowers, the lonely wren
   Warbled its music to the listening glen,
Tender and low as lover's firstborn sigh.
O'er frowning crags, o'er pine-trees towering high,
   East, west, and north, as far as eye could ken,
   O'er leafless woods, deep chasms, and homes of men,
The soft white snows, suntipt, shone placidly.
The groves were bare, yet thus, in white robes drest,
   Landour was lovely as a May-day queen,
Secure, warm, silent as the martin's nest,
   Half hid by lichened rocks and alders green,
What time the clouds shroud Colver's ample breast,
   And northern winds in Deyrah's groves pipe keen.

XLI.

SONNET.

I dreamt I stood beside proud Jericho,
  And saw the sight of Timæus' son restored,
  And heard him bless with loud acclaim the Lord,
And marked the high procession moving slow
Up market place and street ; strange heavy woe
  Pressed on my soul, I longed for one kind word
  From those dear lips ; but on the people poured
Heedless and shouting ; when in accents low,
Sudden I heard the Lord my name call o'er,
  And then with hope I felt my heart endowed,
And reckless of the tumult and uproar,
  And the mad jostlings of the eager crowd,
I rushed with grateful worship to adore,
  And fell down at His feet and wept aloud.

XLII.

SONNET.

CHINI IN KOONAWAR.

Where rugged Meru frowns with brow austere,
  Like a soft strain of soothing harmony,
  By discord rude, beneath a glorious sky,
Warm, azure, radiant, exquisitely clear,
With granite ramparts in her front and rear,
  Lies lonely Chini! the wild cuckoo's cry
  Rings through her spicy groves incessantly,
And plenteous harvests crown her genial year.
Bounded by pine-woods dark, in clover dight,
  Or in gay fern and purple heath arrayed,
Her pastures small, by contrast apposite,
  Seem fairy islands with rich gems inlaid,
Rising 'mid gloomy seas, or circlets bright
  Of stationary sunshine, set in shade.

XLIII.

SONNET.

From a deep rift in slate 'mid Ankhee's snows,
   Gunga leaps up indignant to the light,
   A boisterous torrent, decked with foamballs white
In endless clusters on her dauntless brows ;
The solid rock beneath her ceaseless blows
   Throbs to the centre :—but soon spent with fight,
   She seeks a placid lake, like silver bright,
And sinks exhausted to a calm repose.
Reissuing thence her docile waves pursue,
   Down the broad vale, their course with tranquil mien,
O'er pebbles streaked with veins of softest hue,
   Shaking the laughing flowers and alders green,
And tufts of holly, moist with gleaming dew,
   Where wrens close nestle when the blast is keen.

XLIV.

SONNET.

TERAI—DISTANT PROSPECT OF THE HILLS.

The arching alders with dank moisture shone—
  Above, around, the wild vine, as I past,
  Waved in slow cadence to the fever blast,
Sweeping in fitful gusts with languid moan.
The thick white mist on mouldering stem and stone,
  As evening closed, a fearful shroud rolled fast,
  The blinding darkness round her mantle cast,
And quenched my hopes ere half the woods were won;
A dip! a rise! clean vanished mist and shade,
  And blissful Eden swam at once to sight!
Clear tops of distant hills, a smiling glade,
  And modest farms, blue skies, and pastures bright,
And terraced slopes with grass and flower inlaid,
  Bathed in a flood of autumn's golden light.

XLV.

SONNET.

The flora of the Himalayas, and indeed of all great mountain chains within the tropics, is most varied and extensive.—Hooker's Journal.

On Teesta's slopes bloom flowers of every clime :
   The golden cistus and the 'rath primrose,'
   The dainty crocus, white as Alpine snows,
The azure eyebright and the fragrant thyme,
Daisies as pure as stars in autumn prime,
   And wild musk-roses whose soft leaves expose
   A lovelier crimson than the blush that glows
At early morn on Kanchun's crest sublime;
Blue speedwells, and laburnums burning red,
   And lilies proud, brimful of chaste disdain,
And pansies barred with lines of blackest dye,
And kingcups tender as the evening sky,
And snowdrops pale, "that hang the pensive head"
   Lowly and meek as weeping Madeleine.

XLVI.

SONNET.

RAPIDS OF THE BALASUN.

How would they wrong thy nature, lonely stream,
  Who judging from these leaps, these chidings wild,
  Would think thee restless as a moody child
Tortured with burning pain and feverish dream;
For past these falls, mute as the voiceless steam
  Wafted from green earth after rainfalls mild,
  Thou creep'st with opposition reconciled,
A thread of silver, or a lone sunbeam.
On autumn eves, when faint the north wind blows
  O'er the bleak moors, by leafless covert-side,
E'en the wren's warble suits not thy repose;
  O'er mossy stones so soft thy waters glide,
White nurseling of Dewdanga's stainless snows,
  Joy of the woods, the waste savannah's pride.

XLVII.

SONNET.

(1858.)

While ruthless wars around our cities roll,
    And marts re-echo the wild cry of fear,
    Far from all noise by Teesta's current clear,
Oh for the maple dish and beechen bowl!
The hermit's life, from childhood, was the goal
    Of all my thoughts,—but now the joys severe
    Of the lone cell, hemmed in by mountains drear,
With double power attract my longing soul.
How sweet, while moonlight silvers wood and lawn,
    To 'sleep with upward face,' or pipe at ease;
Or to cull simples ere the meek-eyed dawn
    Hath edged with burning gold the green-robed trees;
Or yet to rove in valleys far withdrawn,
    Cheered by the linnet's song and whispering breeze.

XLVIII.

SONNET.

'Tis sweet at sea reclined on deck to view,
    The seabirds hover to attain the crest
    Of some lone rock, round which the tranquil breast
Of ocean, glimmers like a shield of blue ;
Or watch the fisher in his light canoe,
    When Hesperus, (Eve's eldest born and best,)
    Has lit his circlet in the rosy west,
With swelling sail, afar his course pursue :
Or if green isles lie near, where men abide,
    To note such simple signs of rural life,
As lines of fences amid meadows wide,
    Or lusty herds engaged in playful strife,
By barn and byre o'er which with rapid flight,
Dense flocks of pigeons wheel, like cloudlets white.

XLIX.

SONNET.

IN SUMMER.

At noon I range, equipped with scrip and crook,
    The holt for nuts, or con reclined at ease,
    In the cool shadow of gigantic trees,
Haunted for ages by the social rook,
The legends strange of Spenser's tuneful book,
    Or mark the soaring hawk by slow degrees,
    Melt in the cloudless blue, or watch the bees,
Discourse and labor in their chosen nook :
Or, if the ardent south breathes fervid heat,
    The swimmer's art my limbs with joy essay,
Where bending willows o'er the brooklet meet,
    And rapid swirls clean beds of grit betray,
And salooks sweet their crimson foreheads show,
Mid pliant canes with plumes like virgin snow.

L.

SONNET.

Though far mid glens, with massive boulders strown,
   Where thick at morn and eve the white mists brood,
   Hemmed in by roaring stream and sombre wood,
The blue-eyed Goorkha dwells in peace alone;
Yet is he pleased at times, when winter's flown,
   To saunter leisurely in cheerful mood
   Where Nynee Thal receives its vassal flood,
To view the peaceful church with vines o'ergrown,
The trembling lake, and strips of natural lawn,
   Where the tired herd-boy pipes in careless ease,
   The Christian tombs with tufts of eyebright crowned,
   The pastor's cottage and trim garden ground,
And English farms in lonely dells withdrawn,
   And small white homesteads screened by leafy trees.

LI.

SONNET.

SOURCE OF THE SONE.

As closely sheltered as a land-locked bay,
   Yawns the deep dell, whence slips like crystal clear,
   The infant Sone, to speed past blocks austere,
And scarf green-bosomed slopes in wanton play;
No log built cabins lurk, no shepherds stray
   In this weird rift. The wood that guards its rear,
   Seems a fit spot for cold remorseless Fear,
Auspicious Hope with felon stroke to slay:
And though at noon it hears from glens afar,
   The peasant's shout, and sounding timber wain,
Yet when meek Eve illumes the folding star,
   Profoundest silence claims her right to reign
In every nook, save those where bats let fall,
With short shrill cry, the ripened sâl seedball.

LII.

SONNET.

When wreaths of vapour o'er the brooklet fly,
   And on its border steep unhurt by glare,
   The wild dhatura to the fainting air,
It's chiselled cup of stainless white lifts high,
When keen-eyed owls on noiseless wings go by,
   And gnats remonstrate round my garden chair,
   Behind those trees that skirt the pastures bare,
A circlet bright of lurid light I spy;
Is it a village forge? or watchfire lit
   By careful herdsmen to protect their charge?
Or pyre of faggots round which gipsies sit?
   Or fisher's beacon on the river's marge?
I know not, but for years I nightly mark
That point of lurid light against the dark.

LIII.

SONNET.

Some trees there are whose growth can never fade ;
   Whom nor the woodman's axe nor time can harm ;
   Around their trunks is woven such a charm
Of potent memories. An umbrageous shade
Is ever theirs ; they stand in green arrayed,
   In frosty winter, as when skies are warm ;
   The levin bolt and tempest's wild alarm
Their interlacing branches ne'er upbraid.
Witness the sycamore where Zaccheus sate ;
   The four fraternal yews of Borrowdale ;
The wind-saluted fig by Ilium's gate ;
   The oak where Charles—a weary wight and pale—
Safe from the sullen roundhead's deadly hate,
   Was lulled to sleep by autumn's whispering gale.

LIV.

SONNET.

SACOONTALA.

To him who plods with weary steps and slow,
    Through antique tomes, how fresh these pages seem!
    Not fresher in the wilderness the gleam
Of the cool fountain, round which date palms grow,
And purple stonecrops in rich masses glow,
    To the worn pilgrim, when the noonday beam
    Smites with relentless rage, the jaded team
Of camels that he leads, with head bent low :—
He reads, and summoned by the verse appear,
    The lowly hermitage, and garden small,
Smooth lawns, that slope down to the brooklet clear,
    Bright plots of yellow corn 'mid forests tall,
And peerless maids, in robes of bark that bear
The osier basket, heaped with fruitage rare.

LV.

SONNET.

1871.

O ever first to quell presumptuous pride,
    To dare the despot's wrath and bar his way,
    The impious foes of liberty to slay,—
Of stainless honor, and of valor tried,
O high-souled France! in sadness turn aside,
    From the rude world, in this thy evil day,
    Bend low the knee to God, and weep, and say,—
Thou art my Help, my Confidence and Guide :
'Tis writ, the king who smote Jehovah's foes
    With a continual stroke, who in His sight
Was the Great Hammer of the earth, arose
    From his sad fall arrayed with heavenly might;
Therefore bend low the knee—lift up the eye,
Plead with thy God, O France!—thou canst not die.

LVI.

SONNET.

TO A DOVE.

Fair haunter of the gloomy banyan's bough,
   Whose presence tells that cloudless skies are near,
   That soon the husbandman with carol clear,
And "shining morning face" shall guide the plough,
Dull must the mortal be, and harsh I trow,
   Who dreams no dreams, whom no illusions cheer
   At thy approach, who feels no happy tear
Bedew his eyes, no flush on cheek and brow!
For me, this morn thy murmur like a spell,
   Blots from my eyes the shady banyan tree,
I see instead, the billows sink and swell,
   The Ark slow drifting o'er a shoreless sea,
And thy progenitor its weary way,
Winging in silence with an olive spray.

MISCELLANEOUS PIECES.

ON AN OLD ROMAUNT.

When the night is dark and dreary, and the north wind
    whistles shrill,
And the snow storm drives in fury down the gorges of
    the hill,
Like the necromancer's mirror, when his magic per-
    fumes burn,
Mocking Time, these curious volumes make the glori-
    ous Past return.

Fast as ripples on the river, or cloud-shadows on the
    grass,
As I read their quaint old pages, down my curtained
    chamber pass
Mitred priest, and hospitaller, armed and mounted for
    the fray,
Bands of bronzed condottieri, maidens fair as laughing
    May.

All that fancy loves to cherish, of the grand old feudal times,
Palmer guides, and weary pilgrims, wending home from distant climes,
Trembling Jews with jewel caskets, border chiefs who own no law,
Quivered bands of merry archers, mustered on the 'greené shaw.'

Norman holds, embattled belfrys, gyves, and chains, and dungeons dim,
Winding stairs, and blazing beacons, ancient arms grotesque and grim,
Pensive nuns, in quest of simples, in the lonely midnight hour,
Adepts o'er alembics chanting uncouth rhymes of mystic power.

Foreign marts, Venetian Doges, bales of precious merchandise,
Stately streets in Flemish cities, burgher crowds in peaceful guise,

Mighty dukes by guards attended, foresters in kirtles
    green,
Silver fonts and flaring tapers, ladies sheathed in jewels
    sheen.

Moorish forts in far Grenada, portals barred and tur-
    bans blue,
Gardens green as blissful Eden, crystal fountains fair to
    view,
Divans in the proud Alhambra, fairy mosques of Parian
    stone,
Groups of Moors and whiskered Spaniards, tilting round
    the Soldan's throne.

And enrapt I gaze in silence, like a child before a show,
Heedless in my joy and wonder, how the golden mo-
    ments flow,
Till the cock's shrill ringing clarion breaks the spell and
    clears the air,
And I find me silent seated in my old accustomed chair.

ABSENCE.

1.

When larks are shrilling overhead
    And dewdrops gem each spray,
When o'er the garden's trim-kept walks
    The perfumed breezes play,
When morning floods with light the slope
    Behind the chestnut tree,
I lean against its massy trunk
    And think, my love, of thee.

2.

At noon, when fierce September's sun
    Is blazing in the sky,
And 'neath a golden haze our pools
    And rose-beds quivering lie,
I muse upon the happy hours
    Last autumn when with thee
In careless mood the fields I strayed,
    An angler blithe and free.

3.

When faintly shines the evening star
  Upon our native vale,
And o'er its roof of roseate sky
  The dark rooks slowly sail,
When wains with rich sheaves loaded pass
  The ford beneath the hill,
And shout and merry song are heard,
  My thoughts are with thee still.

4.

When darkness wraps our lowly farm,
  And silence reigns profound,
And merry elves in laughing groups
  The old oak's bole surround,
In peaceful sleep with lightning speed,
  I traverse land and sea,
And view in dreams thy fairy form,
  And converse hold with thee.

REMINISCENCES OF TRAVEL.

THE STRAITS OF JUBAL.

"And mount Sinai was altogether on a smoke."
Exodus 19. 18.

1.

An ardent sun blazed fierce at noon,
  When from the deck I saw,
The holy mount loom on the right,
  Where Israel heard the Law.

2.

No cloud obscured the crystal sky,
  In dazzling beauty spread,
Like some vast temple's shining dome,
  Above its sacred head.

3.

But one dark hern that seemed a speck,
  Against the vault profound,
With outstretched wings and forward neck,
  Wheeled slowly round and round.

4.

The air was dry, the sea was calm,
    The coast so flat and drear,
My naked eyes with ease surveyed,
    The landscape far and near.

5.

The pebbles on the water's marge,
    The wide expanse of sand,
The lone Bedouin that rode afar,
    With shouldered spear and brand.

6.

I gazed, and by the scene inspired,
    My heart recalled the time,
When God himself to mortal men,
    Proclaimed his code sublime.

7.

When Sinai's top was all aflame,
    And wreaths of lurid smoke,
As from a crater's heated mouth,
    Adown its bosom broke.

8.

When on the trackless thirsty waste,
    Untenanted and bare,
Long lines of tents in order stood,
    Whose pennants streamed in air.

9.

When for the stillness deep and dread,
    So oft in deserts found,
Were heard the tread of armèd feet,
    And trumpet's fitful sound.

10.

The ship sailed on, beneath the swell,
    Mount Sinai passed away,
But in my spirit lingers yet,
    The awe I felt that day.

SHADOWS.

I love the uncouth shadows,
    The figures quaint that run,
By bush and hedge when cattle,
    Pass homewards in the sun.

The shadows cast at sunrise,
    By slanting rock and tree,
On lucid pools that tremble,
    My heart leaps up to see.

But most I prize the shadows,
    Which Emma's fingers slight,
For laughing children fashion,
    With subtle skill at night.

When bright the candle shimmers,
    And treble voices call,
For gargoyles on the cornice,
    And rabbits on the wall.

A CHARADE.

1.

Before my First with horse and foot,
    The Duke in leaguer lay,
Huge cannons crowned the slopes around,
    And cruisers watched the bay;
For though the foe was stout of heart,
    The ramparts strong and high,
His Grace had vowed a solemn vow,
    To conquer or to die.

2.

My Second heard the volunteers
    Receive the word to form,
To spring the mine, to launch the bridge,
    And win the breach by storm;
Her nimble hand on sky and air
    Had flung a sable pall,
But soon a lurid light illumed
    The camp and crowded wall.

3.

When Rumour bore on rushing wings
    The startling news to town,
The sheriffs to the victor sent
    A wreath and mural crown;
And let the bonfires blaze, they said,
    And let the church bells toll,
Right valiantly the host hath won
    My first within my whole!

STANZAS.

———

She stood upon a turret high
    To view the deadly fray,
Her dark eyes shaded by her hand,
    Her locks in disarray,
And close beside her knelt her son,
    His cheeks with roses spread,
The while a burning western sky
    Its radiance o'er them shed.

A thousand spears were glancing bright,
    And plumes and flags below
Were streaming in the evening breeze
    Beneath that golden glow;
And blinding was the rocket's flash,
    And loud the cannon's roar,
And distant shouts were frequent heard
    Like waves upon the shore.

Intent she looked—her husband's form
  Where fiercest raged the fight,
Where heaviest hung the lurid smoke,
  Absorbed her aching sight;
A sash of blue was on his breast,
  The symbol of command,
Albania's chosen chief, he led
  That day the Christian band.

' Mark, mother, mark, my father's plume
  Waves proudly in the air.
Oh! if my arm could wield the glaive,
  His peril I would share,
And side by side from foreign yoke
  Defend our natal sod,
Or die a faithful Christian knight
  For country and for God.

' I see, I see his manly form
  Between the closing lines,
A massive cross of burnished gold
  Upon his helmet shines;

He waves his sword, in all the host
   The bravest knight is he!'
The high-souled sinless child exclaimed
   With artless ecstacy.

'Hush, Lyra, hush! Dost hear that shout,
   That echoing trumpet bray?
The Moslem comes, as comes the storm—
   Our bravest bands give way;
The foremost warriors on our side
   Are swept like foam-flakes down,
The foe assails our front and flank,
   Thy father fights alone.'

She saw him fall—she clasped her hands—
   A haze came o'er her eyes:
That night Albania's chieftain met
   His spouse in Paradise.
And firm in faith, though sorely tried,
   Before a month had closed,
Upon the noble orphan's brow
   The martyr's crown reposed.

SOLITUDE.

Nymph, upon whose forehead white
Gleams a wreath of snowdrops bright,
Starred with specks of violets fair,
Meekly peeping here and there,
In the depths of whose clear eyes
Dainty sorrow slumbering lies,
With the new-born Spring come nigh,
Rescue me before I die.

From the city's noise and heat
Lead me to thy green retreat,
Where the wren securely lies,
Hid from prying schoolboys' eyes,
And the sleeping fields and leaves
Dream of Autumn's fruits and sheaves;

Where from valleys far withdrawn,
Sunny slope and thymy lawn,
Bay of hounds and hunters' cheer,
Faintly fall upon the ear.

For the toil and ceaseless strife
Of a townsman's weary life
Tire my spirit and I droop,
Where my betters live in hope;
I am old, oh, think with ruth
How I sought thy face in youth,
Nymph benign! by hidden rills,
In dark lanes, among the hills,
By the plover's dank abode,
On the cheerless mountain road,
By the Banshee's haunted fell,
When at lauds the convent bell,
Softly now,—now full and deep—
Woke the echoes from their sleep.

SUNJOGTA.

'God shield my king!' the damsel said, and waved her small white hand,
Her eye was soft, her brow was fair, none fairer in the land,
And as, amazed, she wildly gazed upon the crowded plain,
The tears rolled down her satin cheeks as fast as wintry rain.

On lucid Jumna's grassy slopes, as far as eye could see,
Like poppy stalks when summer smiles, stood Prithi's chivalry,
Ten thousand horsemen cased in mail that mocked her dark eyes' glance,
With aigrette and with snowy plume, with shield and glittering lance.

Nor lacked there flags and caftans gay ; a hundred banners flew
O'er a hundred haughty barons, broad fringed with gold and blue,
And though her eyes were filled with tears, yet clear against the sky
A myriad scarfs, green, red, and white, Sunjogta could descry.

But o'er that sea of waving silks one glanced supremely tall,
And o'er those files of glimmering crests one brighter shone than all,
And when by trysting tree and scaur that flag and crest swept by,
With loud acclaim young Prithi's name she heard the people cry.

Her heart was sad, her spirit faint, and fearful was the sight
Of spears in rest and prancing steeds and men in armour dight,

But grief and fear she cast aside, and never ceased to pray
To Gouri's lord, when rung that shout, to guard her love alway.

When Ravee's flood with Moorish blood shall be red as the Ŭva flower
That in meek-eyed May blooms glossy gay beside the sacred bower,
Then, Siva, from the Moslem's hate protect our youthful king,
And gong and bell and wreathèd shell thy praise shall loudly ring.

FIRE HUNTERS.

There are no abler adepts in the art
Of woodcraft, than the gentle Gonds, who dwell
In the wild region where the mighty sâl,
The hardy salei, and Briarean saj,
O'erhung with creepers of enormous bulk,
Clothe the soft uplands, and the vales that lie
Round the head waters of the rapid Sone.
Unused to agriculture, and devoid
Of e'en such lore as is required to rear
Cattle or sheep or poultry with success,
They look alone to what their woods supply,—
Gums, berries, honey, wholesome nuts and game,—
To meet their wants, and thus from youth become
Experienced trappers, wary, quick of eye,
And full of rare devices to ensnare,
The game that furnishes their fires with meat.

They often start at eve in knots of four,
Equipped with a slight pole of pliant wood,
From which as from a balance beam depend

FIRE HUNTERS.

A heap of branches,—and an earthen jar
With blazing faggots piled of driest wood.
This strange machine, contrived with simple art,
To cast a flaring light upon the path,
The foremost hunter on his shoulder bears,
And while the second, as he jogs, oft shakes
A rod of iron garnished with ten rings,
That jingle lightly like a bunch of keys,—
The hindmost follow with their hunting poles
Of toughened cane, six yards and more in length.

When near the covert side the jingling sound,
Excites the timid hare, (nay bolder game,)
To scour the precincts, and detect the cause :
It tempts the open, but the occult glare
 Frustrates it's purpose, and it stands agaze :
Till a quick thwack! delivered with just aim,
Cuts short its blank surprise and life at once.

If the sport lasts an hour or two, so rich
Are all the coverts of their woods in game,
The hunters come home with a varied bag
Of hares and porcupines and spotted deer.

A CHARADE.

O lady! cast my *all* away,
    Thy baseless fears resign,
It is not meet misdeeming fears
    Should mar a love like thine;

Fears weaken more affection's flame
    In woman's guileless breast
Than e'er my *first* the morning light,
    My *last* the bright steel crest.

Lord Lindsay's heart is thine alone,
    The gray-haired minstrel swore
And fame reports that Allan Bane
    Is versed in mystic lore.

Oh lady! cast my *all* away,
    Thy baseless fears resign,
It is not meet misdeeming fears
    Should mar a love like thine.

SAMARSI.

Samarsi the bold is the pride of his clan,
But he owns not an acre in broad Rajasthan;
Samarsi the bold is the hope of the true,
But his sporran is empty, his henchmen are few,
For the Moors o'er the Jumna in triumph have come,
And Samarsi the bold is an exile from home.

Though the Moslem now feasts in his hall and his bower,
And the crescent flag flutters from temple and tower,
Though the chase and the forest, the pass and the height,
Are watched by the soldiers by day and by night,
Samarsi the bold is as merry as when
His will was the law in his loved native glen.

For the roebuck still bounds by the dark haunted lake,
And the partridge still springs from the deep tangled brake,

And the perch and the salmon in silv'ry shoals gleam,
At morning and noontide in pool and in stream,
And spite of their warders on hill and on plain
Samarsi can harry his father's domain.

Though an outlaw decreed by the chiefs of the foe,
Samarsi has homage from high and from low,
For the copsewood is heavy by Saloombra park,
And the vale of Banmora at noonday is dark,
And he's ready, aye ready, right firmly to stand
By the wood or the pass with his sword in his hand.

In the cave of Pokurna, beneath the green hill,
Where the throstle keeps time to the soft-crooning rill,
Samarsi at nightfall, unknown to the Moor,
Lights his watch-fire in peace, when his labours are o'er,
And revels in freedom till morning again
Gives the signal to mount and ride down to the plain.

STANZAS.

1.

My love, seek not the help of man
    When perils round thee rise;
The search will outrage hope, I swear,
    By sad experience wise.

2.

The kindest friend, when sore thy need,
    Will scornfully deride;
The wisest will misjudge and wrong,
    And coldly turn aside.

3.

But stern, resolved, though dangers frown,
    Press forward day by day;
God's word is sure, thou canst not fall,
    And naught can bar thy way.

STANZAS.

The sun has set, the Brahmin's bell
    Resounds from shrines afar,
And softly shimmers in the west,
    A single lustrous star.

The distant bark whose swelling sails,
    Like wings of sea-gulls gleam,
Impelled by Zephyr's balmy breath,
    Creeps up the noiseless stream.

Blue smoke of lightest texture curls
    Against the rosy sky,
In spots where hid by darksome woods,
    Mill, thorp, and sheepfold lie.

Around the piles of new-mown hay,
    The cricket's song is heard,
The lotus opens on the pool,
    By ripples softly stirred.

The weak-eyed bat that slept all day,
    Quits now its chosen tree,
And tempts the orchard's nets for nuts,
    Or wheels capriciously.

And from the tangled beds of cane,
    That skirt the pathways white,
Dhaturas pure begemmed with dew,
    Exhale a perfume light.

In this calm hour how sweet to sit
    Upon this wave-worn stone!
And idly watch the ebbing tide,
    In pensive mood alone.

Or pray with heart and voice subdued,
    In every state to be,
As truly placid as this stream,
    That lapses silently.

No. 13, MANICKTOLLA STREET.

1.

Within the city's restless heart
    A modest homestead lies,
It's trim-kept lawns a mossy wall
    Secures from envious eyes.

2.

It's turf is fresh, it's wells are pure,
    And by it's pathways clean,
Braving the city air, the rose
    And jasmin white are seen.

3.

Oh, may my heart be ever like
    This nook so green and fair,
Despite the rude world's breath may love
    And innocence bloom there!

THE MAID OF ROOPNAGORE.

The Emperor Aurungzebe, in the height of his power, made an offer of marriage to the Princess of Roopnagore, who haughtily rejected his suit, saying, that she would rather renounce the throne of her ancestors than be allied to an infidel.—SEIR MUTAQUERIN.

Hear how the maid of Roopnagore
Disdained the friendship of the Moor,
When forth by royal hest there came,
With peers and paladins of fame,
A gay young lordling of degree,
The pride of Moslem chivalry,
To win her from her father's side
To be a Kaffir sovereign's bride.

'Go back, Sir Knight,' she sternly said,
While maiden shame her cheeks dyed red,
'Go back and say, for gems and gold,
For lordly Delhi's guarded hold,

For power, for state, for lands in fee,
An odalisque I ne'er will be,
Nor faith and troth will coldly sell
To him who is an infidel.

'The dun-deer on the mountain's side
May with the panther be allied ;
Compelled by bleak December's weather,
The owl and lark may house together ;
Or yet by spring inspired the dove
May seek the hawk's protecting love ;
But Roopnagore in weal and woe
Shall ever deem the Moor a foe.

' In rich brocade, and jewels sheen,
Rather than shine the Moslem's queen,
Rather than greet a fratricide,
I'd be a simple shepherd's bride,
And take as readily my share
Of rustic toil and rustic care,
As ever lowly Rajpoot swain,
On Mewar's still romantic plain.'

STANZAS.

1.

My true love is a snowdrop bud
    That blooms apart from all,
My true love is a timid wren
    That haunts a lonely wall.

2.

My true love is a pilgrim pale,
    Who, day succeeding day,
Threads silent lanes, and shuns the throng
    That crowds the broad highway.

3.

May Grace and Peace my true love guard,
    Where'er her footsteps roam!
And may she find through Christ at last
    In Paradise a home!

STANZAS.

Two wells of unpretending size,
    Far from my native land,
Lie choked with tufts of noxious weeds
    'Mid burning wastes of sand.

Yet Coosey's stream o'erhung with woods,
    Or Gunga fringed with shells,
Comes less before my spirit's eyes
    Than these deserted wells.

By one at eve, ere yet the stars
    Had decked the blue sky's brow,
Rebecca gave the camels drink
    Four thousand years ago.

At Sychar, by the other's side,
    Weary, athirst, misused,
Beneath the fervid noonday sun
    The Saviour sat and mused.

THE MILL.

Beyond the bend where village maids
    Their linen bleach, the rill,
Upgathers by a massive weir,
    Its strength to work a mill.

One moment's space it seems to stop,
    As if to rest from play,
Then plunges headlong on the wheel,
    A mass of silver spray.

Around the fall, gigantic elms
    Their knotted branches wave,
And willows bend in graceful groups,
    Their silken shoots to lave.

And doves that haunt the miller's door
    To pilfer grain or meal,
Not seldom urged by restless fear,
    In rapid circles wheel.

THE MILL.

The mill-house with its roof of slate,
    And gables quaint and high,
Has that sweet mien of calm decay,
    That charms the painter's eye.

And anglers love the sluice-head pool,
    And oft in rapture pause,
To watch its azure depths that shake,
    Like light transparent gauze.

For mottled eels there slyly lurk,
    Mid grit of golden dye,
And lusty trouts on cloudless noons,
    Pursue the dragon fly.

And naught disturbs the silence deep
    That laps the woods around,
Except the sullen plash of waves,
    And mill-wheel's clacking sound.

LINES.

The sisters sing with thrilling power
From yonder lofty convent tower,
But sweeter sing (I hear and say)
The faithful linnets who last May
Built close beside the bank which bounds
The abbey's trim-kept garden-grounds.
I often pass the pair at morn,
Close nestling on a forkèd thorn;
Beneath them, in a hedgerow green,
Their lonely dwelling lurks half seen,
A wattled gem of beauty rare,
Lined thick with carded wool and hair,
And in its cup, like specks of light,
Gleam tiny eggs of purest white.

DIE WEISZE FRAÜ.

"Though mirrors best adorn a lady's room
Yet you, I see have none, sweet Bertha.....why?"
I'll tell you Maud, my best and earliest friend.
When first we came to dwell in Darnel Chase
Four years ago, this house had not been built,
But on its site the lofty manor stood,
Where the forefathers of my lord had lived
Since Richard Crookback's reign, and though decayed
And tenanted by troops of owls, this pile
Had pleasant rooms: the suite of four that lay
Around this very spot, and overlooked
That slope, my lord selected for my use
When I arrived, and I must freely own
I liked them much, they were perhaps too far
From the domestic offices which lay
On the north-eastern side, but for that fault

The cheerful prospect from their windows made
Abundant recompense, for it embraced
Extensive tracts of cultured land, and woods
Laced by the breakers of the silver sea.

Well,—in this ancient house a sitting room,
(One of the four I occupied,) possessed
A lofty mirror framed in ebony ;
It faced a window in a small recess,
Where oft I came at noon to knit and read.
One frosty day, my lord being out, I sat
In this sequestered nook to watch the lawn,
But chancing for a moment to turn round,
In the great mirror opposite I saw
A stranger's countenance beside my own :
It was surmounted by a curious cape,
Like that which ladies wore in Crookback's time :
Startled, I glanced around to ascertain,
If any visitor had unperceived
Entered the chamber,—no !—the room was clear,
And the door fastened by a massive bar !
Again I scanned the mirror,—there it peered !
With spiteful gaze rivetted on my face !

It stayed one minute full,—then faded off,
And I o'ercome with fear, sunk on the floor.

I lay half stunned sometime, at length the sound
Of wheels and horses in the court beneath,
Occasioned by my lord's return, revived
My prostrate soul, I rose—undid the door,
And rushed downstairs with haste to welcome him.

That eve we left for town, but ever since,
I venture not, like others, to adorn
My sitting room with sheets of shining glass,
Or look into a mirror when alone.

ON BOARD S.S. "RETRIBUTION"

OFF CAPE FIOLANT.

With ensigns spread and shotted guns,
    Where seagulls circle free,
For months we roll, and fling at dusk,
    Red lights on rock and sea.

'Tis ours to watch with sleepless zeal,
    Though fierce the north winds blow,
The white stone forts that crown the cliffs,
    The ships that lurk below.

No cruiser dares dart out in chase,
    While thus before the bay,
We slowly wheel, as wheels in air
    The flame-eyed hawk for prey.

A bank of sand looms close astern,
    Ahead the surf-bound coast,
Yet unconcerned alone we float,
    The eye of England's host.

LINES.

"The night is far spent."—Rom. 13-12.

The stars are dim, the moon shines cold,
 A gentle breeze sweeps o'er the lea,
 And softly falls the rippling sea,
On jutting reef and headland bold.

The chaffinch, eldest child of May,
 Impatient in his nest awakes,
 And with his rustling pinion shakes,
The dew that gems the hawthorn spray.

By mountain paths to pastures new,
 The lonely shepherd leads his flock,
 Light wreaths of mist on stream and rock,
Spread filmy veils of softest blue.

O ye, who through the slow-paced night,
 Have watched and wept, lift up your eyes,
 Soon shall the golden morning rise,
And crown the eastern hills with light.

SITA.

चन्द्रागोचितां सीतां रक्तचन्दनसेविनीम् ।
वर्षमुष्णाच्च शीतच्च नेष्यथाय्रु विवर्णताम् ॥

Ramayún.

1.

For vest of vair,
Oh lady fair,
Bark mantles robe thee now,
Rudrakhis brown
Replace the crown
That bound thy queenly brow.

2.

For walks ere dawn,
O'er clean swept lawn,
Thy feet thread wastes to bring,
When noon's fierce eye,
Burns earth and sky,
The pitcher from the spring.

3.

Thy fingers white,
That touched so light,
The lute at fall of day,
With pain at eve,
Green rushes weave,
Beneath the taper's ray.

4.

Yet chase all fear,
Is He not near
To shield, to help, to bless,
Whose love faints not
Who ne'er forgot
The righteous in distress.

THE BROOK.

Beneath a cliff from which at dawn
    A pair of eagles sally,
This gentle streamlet springs from earth,
    To sparkle down the valley.

Basaltic rocks for one short league
    O'erhang it's tiny billows,
And then come shelving banks of turf,
    Adorned with weeping willows.

And fairy isles where timid wrens,
    Their anthems sweetly warble,
And herons stand so stiff and still
    They seem of Parian marble.

The shepherd seeks it's shady marge,
    When noon the landscape hushes,
To slumber in it's coverts cool,
    Or plait its pliant rushes.

The gipsy maid with lustrous eyes,
    And wealth of raven tresses,
Explores with naked feet it's pools,
    To fill her scrip with cresses.

And truant lads with rod and line,
    It's mazes wild unravel,
To lure the lusty trouts that haunt
    It's bed of golden gravel.

Past mill and thorp, past fold and farm,
    It sweeps, yet still it's current,
Contracts no sordid stains to mar
    It's purity inherent.

And as the righteous soul meets death,
    Unruffled by commotion,
E'en so it meets in peaceful mood
    The dark abyss of ocean.

COCO PALMS.

WRITTEN ON A SLAB OF STONE AT GALLE.

This grove on the edge of the limitless ocean,
That watches forever the rhythmical motion,
   Resistless as Fate of it's bosom profound ;

Is silent at noon like a temple forsaken,
Or grotto gigantic whose echoes awaken,
   If crickets but chirp with a tremulous sound :

But grandly at sunset, when gnats pipe in chorus,
It welcomes the south wind with peans sonorous,
   And scatters its ripe nuts by scores on the ground.

MARGARETE.

" Du bist's! O sag es noch ein mal."—Goethe.

I hold thee,—and the dungeon walls,
    The pallet-bed and chain,
Dissolve and fade, as fades the snow,
    In April's genial rain.

I see instead, the busy street,
    Before the sacred shrine,
Where first one morn (oh happy chance!)
    My glance encountered thine.

The garden too, starts up revealed,
    The rustic seat,—the tree,
That heard us vow with lifted hands,
    Eternal constancy.

Oh speak! the magic of thy tone,
    Shall soothe each anxious care,
And nerve anew my prostrate soul,
    To combat with Despair.

WATER FOWL.

From the low hills that skirt these mighty meres,
And more than rival in their loveliness
The dreaming Indian's Happy hunting grounds,
In boyhood's careless prime, I once beheld
The wild fowl migrate. 'Twas a cloudless morn
In early spring; the sun had bathed in gold
The dew-sprent turf, and trees of giant girth,
Whose gnarlèd trunks, deep scarred and scathed with fire,
Raised by the neighbouring herdsmen to destroy
The rotting leaves, and withered undergrowth,
And clear the pastures for the early grass,
Stood like grim warders of the lone hill side
On which I lay,—a faint breeze stirred the leaves,
When from the fens a mighty rushing sound
Rose,—the precursor of a wedge-shaped host
Of swans, and pelicans, and clamorous geese,
White-collared teals, widgeons, and stately cranes
With flecks of vivid green upon their wings.
Northwards the phalanx streamed, and soon the sky
Was hid as with a veil of glancing wings!

And from the grassy slope my wondering eyes
Could at one single glance, with ease, survey
Myriads of birds! for hours and hours they flew,
With harsh shrill screams that echoed from the woods.

It was a sight to fire with wild delight
A youthful heart. I felt a keener joy
Than feels in far Caffrarian wilds the Boer,
(Lone tenant with his partner of a hut
And cherished garden 'mid the arid waste,)
At a "trek bokken," when the nimble deer
Sweep past his tiny farm, in such vast herds,
That to the welkin's verge the brown karroo
Seems a bright carpet to the gazer's eye.

Long years have past of joys and griefs and cares
Since that spring morn of which I speak, yet oft,
When I sit silent in long winter eves,
And gaze upon the fire in listless mood,
To my mind's eye return in vision clear,
Those gnarlèd trunks upon the lone hill side,
That cloud of outstretched necks and restless wings!

NEAR SEONI.

Sweet brook! with thy exhaustless store
    Of cool translucent water,
Which Brahmins for libations pour,
    When altars reek with slaughter,
Dost thou not typify the life
    Of saints devout and lowly,
Whose course undimmed by stains or strife,
    Is tranquil, bright, and holy?

NOTES.

XVIII.—*Sonnet* (Khan Saheb's House, College Square), page 18.

"A Persian's mansion near the Vacool trees."

The Vacool is the Mimusops Elengi, a large timber tree remarkable for the delightful fragrance of its flowers. There are splendid specimens of this tree in the College green, Potuldanga, and in the gardens of the Taj at Agra, as also in the enclosed gardens of the palace at Deeg.

XX.—*Sonnet* (Gibraltar), page 20.

"As on the day when baffled France and Spain,
Beheld their vaunted ships in flames ashore," &c.

The grand attack during the great siege was made on the 12th September 1782. Col. Drinkwater in his interesting account says, "the ten battering ships after leaving the men-of-war, wore to the north, and a little past nine o'clock bore down in admirable order to their several stations." &c. &c. "For some hours the attack and defence were so equally supported, as scarcely to admit of any appearance of superiority in the cannonade on either side." The number of heavy guns engaged was 96 on the part of the garrison, and 142 on the part of the enemy, in their floating batteries alone. "The wonderful construction of the ships seemed to bid defiance to the powers of the heaviest ordnance. Even the artillery themselves, at this period, had their doubts of the effects of the red hot shot, jocularly termed by the men " roasted potatoes," which began to be used about twelve, but were not general till between one and two o'clock. In the afternoon however the face of things began to change considerably, the smoke which had been observed to issue from the upper part of the flagship, appeared to prevail, notwithstanding the constant application of water, and the admiral's second was perceived to be in the same condition. Confusion was now apparent on board several of the vessels, and by evening their cannonade considerably abated ; about 7 or 8 o'clock it almost totally ceased. Our artillery at this period must have caused dreadful havoc amongst them. An indistinct clamour, with lamentable cries and groans, proceeded from all quarters, and a little before midnight a wreck floated in under the town line wall."

XXII.—*Sonnet* (Aboukir), page 22.

"Then rose in air the battle's dreadful roar,
The guns flashed fiercely from each blood-stained deck."

The battle of the Nile was fought on the 1st August 1798. Nelson used to call it a conquest not a victory. Says an English writer, "the vastly superior forces of the French, and the strength of their position, (protected towards the north by dangerous shoals, and towards the west by the castle and batteries,) led Admiral Brueys to consider that position impregnable, and on the strength of this conviction, he wrote to Paris that Nelson had purposely avoided him. Was he undeceived, when Hood in the *Zealous* made signal that the enemy was in sight, and a cheer of triumph burst from every ship in the British fleet? That fleet which had swept the seas with bursting sails for six long weeks, in search of its foe, and now bore down upon him with fearless exultation." Mr. James in his Naval History states, that "the rapidity and precision with which the British fleet formed line, elicited the admiration of the French, the more so, on account of the pell mell state in which the ships had previously bore down. Soon after the British had thus formed they hoisted their colours, and sulsequently union jacks in several parts of their rigging ⁂ As the ships streamed in, a prompt and well directed broadside from the *Zealous*, brought down by the board the *Guerriere's* foremast. The sun was at this moment sinking into the horizon, and not a British ship except the *Zealous* had yet fired a shot. So auspicious a commencement of the attack, was greeted with three cheers by the whole British fleet."

XLIX.—*Sonnet* (In Summer), page 49.

"And salooks sweet their crimson foreheads show."

Salook (Nymphea Rubra). "Native of India, very handsome when in blossom, with its large and brilliant red flowers."
Firminger's Gardening in India.

LI.—*Sonnet* (Source of the Sone), page 51.

"The ripened Sal seedball."

Sal (Shorea Robusta.) "The principal timber tree in the eastern parts of Central India. Yields the dammer resin of commerce. Seeds eaten by wild tribes."—*Forsyth's* "*Highlands of Central India.*"

NOTES.

LII.—*Sonnet*, page 52.
"And on its border steep unhurt by glare
The wild Dhatura to the fainting air."

The night-blowing Dhatura Alba, is a common wayside weed, conspicuous for its large handsome flowers. Bishop Heber in his "Evening Walk" happily says, that it's blossom is:

"Of fragrant scent and virgin white
A pearl upon the locks of night."

LV.—*Sonnet* (1871), page 55.
"To dare the despot's wrath and bar his way."

Sings the greatest of living poets :

C'est l'ange de nuit.
Rois, il vous suit
Marquant d'avance
Le fatal moment
Au firmament.
Son nom est France
Ou chatiment.
(Victor Hugo, *Les Chatiments.*)

Sunjogta, page 75.
"Is red as the Uva flower."

The uva is the Hibiscus. The gardens of India are very rich in the handsome species of this genus that they contain. It is a flower of peculiar sanctity among the Hindus.

Fire Hunters, page 78.
"The hardy Salei and Briarean Saj."

The salei is a very common tree in all parts of Central India. Its wood is useless as timber, but it is very hardy, and grows well from stakes planted during the monsoons. It yields plentifully the fragrant gum resin called *labanu*, long supposed to be the olibanum used as incense by the ancients. It is used as such now in Hindu temples. The saj is one of the best timbers of the second class, much used for building and all common purposes—bark used for tanning. Tusser silk worm lives on the leaves.—*Forsyth's "Highlands of Central India."*

Sita, page 99.
"Rudrakhis brown."

Rudrakhis are the seeds of the Elæocarpus Ganitrus. They are commonly strung and worn like beads, and held in much esteem by the orthodox in all parts of India.

www.ingramcontent.com/pod-product-compliance
Lightning Source LLC
Chambersburg PA
CBHW031348160426
43196CB00007B/771